SOLVING SCIENCE MYSTERIES

# Why Does Sound Travel?

## All About Sound

**Nicolas Brasch**

T0044378

**PowerKiDS** press.

New York

Published in 2010 by The Rosen Publishing Group, Inc.
29 East 21st Street, New York, NY 10010

Produced and designed by Denise Ryan & Associates
Editor: Helen Moore and Edwina Hamilton
Designer: Anita Adams
Photographer: Lyz Turner-Clark
U.S. Editor: Joanne Randolph

Photo Credits: p. 6 top: Thad Zajdowicz; p. 6 bottom: © Photographer: Kathy Wynn | Agency: Dreamstime.com; pp. 7, 16 top, 17, 18 top and 19: Photolibrary; p. 8: Tomasz Pietryszek; p. 9 Nellie Buir; p. 11 top: © Photographer: Pavel Losevsky | Agency: Dreamstime.com; p. 11 middle: Afonso Lima; p. 11 bottom: © 2009 Photographer Scott Suchmani /The John F. Kennedy Center for the Performing Arts; p. 12 top: James Steidl; p. 12 middle: DK Images; p. 12 bottom: © Photographer: Javarman | Agency: Dreamstime.com; p. 13 top: © Photographer: Curtpick | Agency: Dreamstime.com; p. 14 top: Courtesy Michael Murphy; p. 15 top: Sharon Dominick; p. 15 bottom: Courtesy Jeff Busby; p. 16 bottom: Jean Scheijen; p. 18 bottom: © Photographer: Paul Cowan | Agency: Dreamstime.com; p 22 top © www. iStockphoto.com/William Mahnken; p. 22 bottom © www.iStockphoto.com/Wojciech Gajda.

Library of Congress Cataloging-in-Publication Data

Brasch, Nicolas.
  Why does sound travel? : all about sound / Nicolas Brasch.
    p. cm. — (Solving science mysteries)
  Includes index.
  ISBN 978-1-61531-888-9 (lib. bdg.) — ISBN 978-1-61531-908-4 (pbk.) —
ISBN 978-1-61531-909-1 (6-pack)
  1. Sound—Miscellanea—Juvenile literature. 2. Noise—Miscellanea—Juvenile literature. I. Title.
  QC225.5.B73 2010
  534—dc22
                            2009031076

Manufactured in the United States of America

CPSIA Compliance Information: Batch #WW10PK: For Further Information contact Rosen Publishing, New York, New York at 1-800-237-9932

# Contents

# Questions About Sound and Noise

## Q: What is sound?

**A:** Sounds are **vibrations** that travel through the air or another **medium**, such as water, and can be heard. As they travel, they change the pressure of the medium through which they travel. This is what causes the noise. Sound travels in waves and the volume of a sound depends on the size, height, and frequency of the waves it creates.

*sound waves*

# Q: How do our ears hear sound?

A: Our ears have three main sections. These are the outer ear, the middle ear, and the inner ear. The outer ear collects sound waves as they pass by. These waves are then channeled into the middle ear, where they hit the eardrum. The resulting vibrations move into the inner ear where they are converted into signals that are sent to the brain.

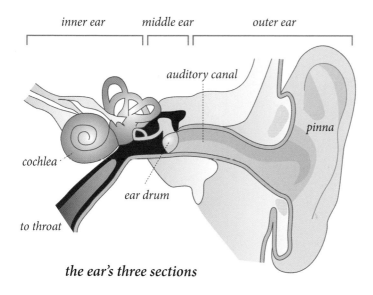

*inner ear*  *middle ear*  *outer ear*

*auditory canal*

*pinna*

*cochlea*

*ear drum*

*to throat*

**the ear's three sections**

# Q: How do you measure how loud something is?

A: The volume of a sound is measured in **decibels** (dB). Decibels are graded on a decibel scale. The lowest point of the scale is 0. The lowest point at which a human ear can detect a sound is 10. A jet aircraft flying overhead registers at about 130 on the decibel scale. The loudest rock bands in the world can create sounds about 150 dB in strength.

## Q: How does soundproofing work?

**A:** Soundproofing **involves** placing special objects where they can prevent or **decreases** the noise that reaches a particular spot. When sound waves hit an object, some of the sound is **absorbed** by it, while the rest of the sound **bounces** somewhere else. The **materials** that are used for soundproofing, such as wool and foam, are highly **absorbent**.

*air pocket*

*glass pane*

### Double Glazing

Double glazing is used to soundproof homes and offices. Two panes of glass are pressed together with air space between them. Most noise bounces off the first pane of glass. Any noise that gets through the first pane is absorbed by the air pocket or is too weak to get through the second pane of glass.

< *These soundproofing pyramids are made from carbon and other materials.*

7

# Questions About Sound and Speed

## Q: Why does the sound of a car change as it passes by?

A: When a car is moving, the sound waves from the engine are farther apart behind the car than they are in front of the car. The movement of the car pushes the sound waves in front of it closer together and the sound waves behind it are stretched out. So, when a car is approaching someone, they will hear the high **pitch** from the bunched-up sound waves. Then, when the car passes them, they hear the lower pitch from the spread out sound waves. This is known as the Doppler effect.

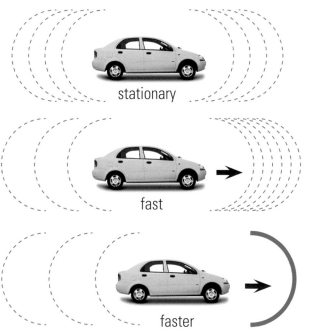

stationary

fast

faster

# Q: Why do I hear thunder after I have seen lightning?

A: Thunder is caused by lightning, although they both occur at exactly the same time. The reason you hear the sound of thunder after you see the lightning is because light travels much faster than sound. The speed of light is almost 1,864,113 miles per second (3,000,000 km/s), while the speed of sound is only 1,115 feet per second (340 m/s). So the light reaches our eyes much faster than the sound reaches our ears.

# Questions About Sound and Deflection

## Q: Why are echoes only loud and clear sometimes?

A: Sound waves are like other energy waves, such as light. When they hit a surface, they are **deflected** and bounce off it. However, they bounce off some surfaces much better than others. The harder and smoother a surface is, the more powerful the bounce will be. So, when someone yells in an empty corridor or in a cave, the sound bounces loud and clear off the walls. Sound waves bouncing into a soft surface, such as a pillow, will be absorbed.

# Q: Are concert halls specially designed for sound?

A: Only some of the sound that is heard at a concert comes directly from the stage. The rest comes from the sound waves that are **reflected** from the walls and ceiling. So, the walls and ceiling must be hard and smooth. Listeners do not want to hear echoes, so soft and curved objects are set up to absorb some of the sound.

*The Kennedy Center Concert Hall, Washington, D.C.*

# It's a Fact

## > Loudest Animal Sound

The loudest sound made by an animal is the grunt of a blue whale. It can reach more than 180 dB and be heard more than 497 miles (800 m) away.

## > Loudest Noise

The loudest noise heard by humans was the volcanic eruption of Krakatau in Indonesia in 1883. The noise was heard more than 2,858 miles (4,600 km)

## > Sound as a Weapon

The blue whale's grunt is not just a method of communication. It is also a weapon. The sound stuns fish, which the whale then feeds on.

## > A Batty Fact

Bats navigate by sound, rather than sight. They make noises and then listen to the echoes to work out how close they are to objects.

## > Sound and Temperature

Sound waves travel more slowly in cold weather than they do in warm weather.

## > In One Ear . . .

Sounds reach one ear a fraction of a second before they reach the other. This helps people locate which direction a sound is coming from.

## > Pain in the Ears

Exposure to a noise of 140 dB or higher can cause immediate damage to a person. Even listening to a noise of 110 dB for just one minute can cause permanent damage.

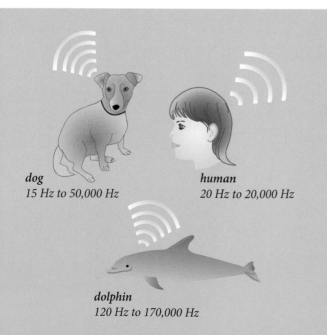

*dog*
*15 Hz to 50,000 Hz*

*human*
*20 Hz to 20,000 Hz*

*dolphin*
*120 Hz to 170,000 Hz*

## Sound and Frequency

The closer sound waves are to each other, the higher the pitch of the sound. Pitch is measured in **hertz** (Hz). While humans can hear sounds up to 20,000 Hz, dogs can hear sounds up to 50,000 Hz. Dolphins can hear sounds up to 170,000 Hz.

# Can You Believe It?

## Breaking the Sound Barrier

When an aircraft travels faster than the speed of sound, it creates a huge "boom." This is because the aircraft pushes air away at such a rate that waves of air build up and crash into one another.

The sound of a whip cracking is caused by the same effect: the end of the whip is moving faster than the speed of sound.

## Sound Pictures

Sound engineers who work for TV, radio, and movies have to make a "sound picture" for a complete scene. If the script calls for stampeding horses, they often have to make the beat of hooves, add splashing water as the horses rush through a river, and a muffled thud as they reach the riverbank.

## Shattering a Glass

A crystal glass will shatter if it is exposed to a sound that has a particular pitch and volume for a long enough period of time. When the noise first occurs, the glass vibrates. If the sound continues long enough, the glass will shatter. So, an opera singer who can hold a high note for a long time could shatter a glass.

# Who found out?

## Doppler Effect: Christian Doppler

Austrian **physicist** Christian Doppler (1803–1857) discovered that the distance between sound waves varies when coming from a moving object. After proposing this **theory**, he tested it by having two trumpeters play the same note at a train station.

One was standing still, while the other was on a moving train. Doppler found that the sound made by each trumpeter was different. This effect is now known as the Doppler effect.

# Inventor of the Telephone: Alexander Graham Bell

The Scottish inventor Alexander Graham Bell (1847–1922) is usually credited with inventing the telephone. His mother was hearing impaired and Bell worked as a teacher to other hearing-impaired people.

In the 1870s, he set about inventing a device that would **transmit** speech along wires. He did this by finding a way to turn the sound waves of speech into electrical signals that exactly matched the pattern of the sound waves and that could travel along wires.

# Bat Scientist:
## Lazaro Spallanzani

The Italian scientist Lazaro Spallanzani (1729–1799) observed that bats **navigated** well in the dark. He began to wonder whether bats used their eyes or another part of their body to guide them.

At first he conducted some experiments that involved blinding the bats and found that they still navigated perfectly. He then filled their ears with wax and observed them flying into walls. Spallanzani's experiments led to an understanding of how bats use echoes to guide them.

*A fruit bat in flight*

# Mach 1: Chuck Yeager

The American pilot Chuck Yeager (1923– ) was the first person to fly an aircraft faster than the speed of sound. Before Yeagar achieved this **feat**, scientists were unsure exactly what would happen at the point that this occurred. They feared that it could cause an aircraft to break up and crash. But on October 14, 1947, Yeager powered his aircraft faster than the speed of sound (known as Mach 1) and landed safely, but only after creating a "boom" that scientists now know is a result of waves of air crashing into each other.

# It's Quiz Time!

The pages where you can find the answers are shown in the red circles, except where otherwise noted.

## Find the odd one out

1. middle ear  inner ear    outer ear   central ear   (5)

2. drinking glass plastic cup    mug    paper cup   (15)

3. pillow    curtain     cave wall   cloth   (10)

## Choose the correct words

1. When sound waves hit a surface, they (slip, bounce, jump) off it.   (7)

2. The (moan, scream, grunt) of a blue whale is the loudest sound made by an animal.   (12)

3. Alexander Graham Bell invented the (megaphone, telephone, microphone).   (17)

## Sounds Good

| N | V | J | Z | X | H | V | G | U | F |
|---|---|---|---|---|---|---|---|---|---|
| A | N | J | T | G | C | Z | Q | O | R |
| V | I | B | R | A | T | I | O | N | D |
| I | Y | F | C | R | I | R | O | E | H |
| G | Z | E | E | Y | P | H | C | G | H |
| A | M | H | M | D | Q | I | Q | Y | M |
| T | A | M | N | U | B | B | Q | K | E |
| E | S | U | T | E | L | B | N | U | G |
| M | O | S | L | B | R | O | S | B | A |
| S | D | U | P | M | V | Z | V | I | N |

## Find these words

There are eight of them.

Absorb

Soundproof

Decibel

Vibration

Hertz

Volume

Navigate

Pitch

# Try It Out!

Do you remember reading that sounds are vibrations on page 4? Now we are going to put that idea into action. Have fun being a sound scientist!

## What You'll Need:
toilet paper tube, paper towel tube, wax paper, rubber band

## What to Do:

Place a piece of wax paper over one end of your toilet paper tube. Fix it in place with the rubber band. Next put your mouth on the other end of the tube and hum. What happens? The sound waves you sent through the tube caused the paper to vibrate!

## Now Try This!

Say something out loud. Now say it again through a paper towel tube. Does it sound different? Try talking through tubes of different lengths and see what happens.

# Glossary

**absorbed** (ub-SORBD) Soaked up.

**absorbent** (ub-SOR-bent) Able to soak up efficiently.

**bounces** (BOWNS-ez) Springs up, down, or to the side.

**decibels** (DEH-seh-belz) Units for measuring the loudness of sound.

**decrease** (dih-KREES) To get smaller or less.

**deflected** (dih-FLEK-ted) Changed direction.

**feat** (FEET) An achievement or triumph.

**hertz** (HURTS) The measurement of the number of sound waves passing by a particular point in one second.

**involves** (in-VOLVZ) Includes something.

**materials** (muh-TEER-ee-ulz) What things are made of.

**medium** (MEE-dee-um) A thing through which something moves.

**navigated** (NA-vuh-gayt-ed) Found the way.

**physicist** (FIH-zeh-sist) Someone who studies physics. Physics is the way things act and react.

**pitch** (PICH) The highness or lowness of a sound.

**reflected** (rih-FLEK-ted) Thrown back or cast back.

**theory** (THEE-uh-ree) An idea.

**transmit** (tranz-MIT) To send out a signal.

**vibrations** (vy-BRAY-shunz) Repeated movements.

# Index

**A**
air, 4, 7, 14
aircraft, 6, 14, 19

**B**
Bell, Alexander
    Graham, 17
brain, 5

**D**
deflection, 11
Doppler, Christian, 16
Doppler effect, 8, 16
    Graham, 17

**E**
ears, 5–6, 13
echoes, 10–12, 18

**F**
frequency, 4

**I**
inventor, 17

**L**
light, 9–10
lightning, 9

**N**
note, 15–16

**P**
pitch, 8, 13, 15

**R**
reflection, 11

**S**
scientist(s), 18–19
soundproofing, 7
sound waves, 4–5,
    7–8, 10–11, 13,
    16–17, 22
Spallazani, Lazaro, 18
speed, 9, 19

**T**
thunder, 9

**V**
vibrations, 4–5, 15, 22
volume, 4, 6, 15

**Y**
Yeager, Chuck, 19

# Web Sites:

Due to the changing nature of Internet links, PowerKids Press has developed an online list of Web sites related to the subject of this book. This site is updated regularly. Please use this link to access the list: *www.powerkidslinks.com/ssm/travel/*